The Little Ang

MW00981560

The Angel Told Me to Tell You Good-bye

Written & Illustrated

by Leia A. Stinnett

ISBN 0-929385-84-5

Published by
StarChild Press
a division of
Light Technology
Publishing
P.O. Box 1526
Sedona, Arizona 86339
(520) 282-6523

Printed by
**MISSION
POSSIBLE**
Commercial
Printing
P.O. Box 1495
Sedona, AZ 86339

The Angel Told Me to Tell You Good-bye

A Little Boy's Experience with Death

A Special Introduction

Boys and girls . . . my name is Anya. I have just arrived on Earth at the dawning of this new age. I have come to present to you wonderful stories, meditations and exercises that you can work with at home. They will help you better understand yourselves and some of the experiences you may be going through now, or those

you are about to encounter in the near future.

How do you feel about death? Are you afraid of death? Do you feel that when you die, you are alone in some dark place, or once you die, that's it? It's all over? Or do you feel good about death and know you will return to Earth again?

The story I am about to share with you is about a little boy, Timmy, who is dying. I am sure you will enjoy his experience and the lesson he learned from his guardian angel, which he shared with those he loved before he left the Earth.

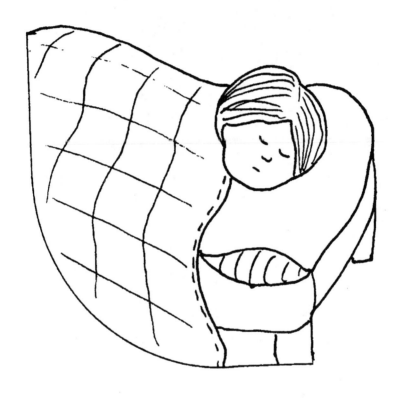

Timmy lay quietly, snuggled under the loving folds of the big, colorful comforter Grandma had made for him just before she passed away two years ago.

Now Timmy was passing away — dying. "There is no hope — no hope at all!" The doctor's words kept repeating over and over in his head, like a scratched phonograph record.

The frail little boy refused to accept his fate. He was afraid to die.

What would it be like? . . . All dark and so cold. And, Timmy thought, "I won't ever

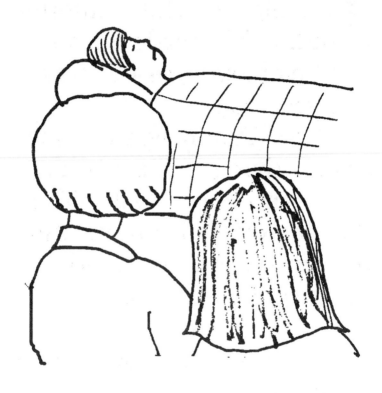

see Mommy and Daddy again!"

Timmy's sobbing became louder. He did not want to die. Why did *he* have to die?

He couldn't think of any reason why God was taking him away from his parents, his friends, all the people he loved. Was he so naughty he deserved to die?

He was only a little boy, he thought — only nine years old.

"Why can't I live to be old like Grandma was when she died? Why do I have to leave now?"

Timmy's parents were having a very difficult time accepting Tim's illness and

coming death. Their small, two-bedroom home – once filled with warmth, love and laughter – was now stilled by the cloud of sadness and hopelessness they felt over their son's illness.

Mom and Dad would quietly tiptoe into Timmy's room several times a day, sit at his bedside and look into each other's eyes, as if to ask, "What can we do to help Tim?"

Tim's mom would cry almost the very minute she would come into the room. Every now and then, Timmy would catch a glimpse of a tear shimmering down his father's cheek as well.

His parents' reactions to his illness only made Timmy feel worse. He was so very sick and in so much pain. Yet he felt it was his responsibility to stay here on Earth, to make his parents happy.

He did not want them to be sad, to cry all the time, and he really did not want to leave. "Mom and Dad will be happy again if I stay, even if I am sick," Timmy rationalized.

One night as Timmy lay in his bed, almost asleep and thinking about what death would really be like, a golden white light appeared at his bedside. The light grew larger and larger . . . brighter and

brighter . . . until it nearly filled the entire room.

Timmy pulled the covers up under his nose so only his big, blue eyes and the top of his head were visible to the intense light. Before Timmy's very eyes a beautiful lady appeared, but this was not an ordinary lady.

Tim noticed something very special about her besides her beautiful skin, rosy cheeks and long, golden hair.

She had wings — big, golden wings! "Who are you?" Tim shuddered, peeking out from behind his comforter.

"I am Sarah, your guardian angel," said the woman with

wings in a soft, melodic voice. "I am here to show you that death is nothing to fear, that it really is a very beautiful experience — a time to rest before you come back to Earth to live another lifetime."

"Come back?" Tim asked, puzzled at what the angel had just said. "Come back?"

"Yes, come back," said Sarah. "Be still. I will show you," assured the angel of light.

Very slowly, Timmy began to relax, and the covers soon melted from around his face. He could feel a tremendous love from this angel, a love directed right at him.

Timmy had never felt this

type of love before — so perfect, so intense, so incredibly different from the love he experienced from his family and friends.

No matter how angry he felt, how afraid, how unattractive, Sarah continued to send him this wonderful feeling of love. The love made Timmy feel very special.

"Close your eyes, Timmy. I will touch my hand to your forehead, and you will be able to see pictures of what takes place when you die, or 'pass over' as I prefer to call the experience.

"You will see a very

beautiful place where you will go to rest after death until it is time for you to come back to Earth. You will see for yourself, there is nothing to fear because death is really a very special and beautiful experience," said Sarah.

Timmy felt a little anxious, but oh, so excited about this new adventure.

"Oh, my!" Timmy exclaimed.

He suddenly realized when the angel appeared in his room, he didn't feel so bad. Maybe the angel could make him well again. He would ask her if she could.

Sarah touched Timmy's forehead ever so gently. He

felt a rush of warm, loving energy penetrate his forehead and travel through his entire body, like water flowing through a tiny creek bed. He had never had this feeling before. He felt he was floating, quietly floating.

Then the first picture appeared in his mind.

Timmy saw his physical body laying very still on the bed, his mom and dad holding and rocking his body in their arms as they cried. This picture made Timmy sad.

Then Tim could see himself in a very different body — a clear, white, transparent body. He was fascinated with

his new body.

Tim felt he looked the same as he did in his old body, but he could sense everything so much better. And what he especially liked was that he could move through walls without even opening the door.

Tim floated higher and higher, far and above the roof of his house. He soared high above the treetops and out into what appeared to be the universe.

As he passed through a colorful tunnel of lights, he was drawn into a beautiful garden full of lush green trees and colorful flowers. He could feel himself being

pulled suddenly toward a crystal bridge that glistened in the bright sunlight.

The bridge seemed to dance with every color of the rainbow. The bridge made Timmy feel like dancing.

Timmy stopped just before crossing the bridge. Something told him to move forward. Perhaps he was afraid of what he would find on the other side.

As he gazed across the bridge from his vantage point, he saw in the brilliant light a familiar face — his beloved grandmother.

And then he saw Uncle Jack and Aunt Fay, two of his

favorite relatives.

"Grandma, Grandma," Tim shouted with joy. "Uncle Jack! Aunt Fay! You're alive! You've been here in this garden all along. How come you didn't tell me where you were? Why haven't you called? I've missed you!"

"No, Timmy," Grandma said softly. "We have passed on. We are in a very beautiful place where we are happy. We never have to be sad, angry or feel sickness and pain."

"There is only one feeling here — love! We are always happy, healthy and loving."

"Gee!" Tim exclaimed.

"Sounds like a great place! Can I visit? And you look different. You all look so beautiful . . . so young. Oh, I didn't mean *you*, Uncle Jack. You look especially handsome."

Sarah stepped into the picture now.

"Tim, you may only go as far as the middle of the bridge. The rest of the journey will be a special surprise for you when you are ready to leave Earth," Sarah warned him.

"But you will be able to see and learn enough to make you feel more comfortable about death and what you will experience as you go through

the process yourself."

Sarah's voice was reassuring.

Slowly, reluctantly, Timmy began to cross the crystal bridge, Sarah holding his hand.

Sarah led Timmy to the middle of the bridge while Grandma encouraged him to come forward.

Tim saw a huge and what would appear to be a blinding white light on the other side of the bridge next to a hill covered with golden daisies.

As Tim looked into the light, he found to his surprise that rather than hurting his eyes, the light seemed to massage, to soothe them, to help Tim relax.

In a moment, Tim saw Jesus, dressed in a long, white robe and smiling lovingly at Tim.

"Timmy, I will wait for you here at this very spot when you are ready to leave Earth and join your grandma and aunt and uncle. I know you are a little afraid of death, but I will be here to take your hand.

"You are not alone now, and you will not be alone when you die. You will be happy and healthy again.

"I love you very much, and I am glad you love me, too. Remember I will wait for you here!" And Jesus touched Timmy's cheek.

Timmy's face took on an intense golden glow. In fact, his whole body was now glowing in light. He felt no fear, no sadness — only love!

He knew death was no big, deep, dark mystery. He knew now, death was not full of sadness and pain. Death was not something to fear as he had once believed.

Sarah stepped back into Tim's picture. "Timmy, I told you earlier tonight that I would explain to you what I meant when I said, 'You come back to Earth to live in other lifetimes.' Look! I will show you what I mean."

Timmy was shown a lifetime

he had lived as a Roman soldier. Sarah pointed out to him that in this lifetime his mother was his brother and his father was his son.

Sarah explained to him how we can experience a new lifetime with the same people we lived our past lifetimes with, but they would appear many times in a different role and in a different body.

Sarah pointed out that when we live again and again, we can be a boy in one lifetime and a girl in another, depending on the type of life we choose to live.

Timmy saw a picture where he had been a Chinese princess.

"Gosh, I was a girl," he said to Sarah, a bit disgusted with this realization.

Sarah smiled and nodded. He also saw himself as a soldier, fighting for the North in the Civil War. "Yes, I was real close to Abe Lincoln, President Abe Lincoln," Tim said with a proud grin on his face.

Even with all these exciting visions, Timmy became very sullen and withdrawn for a moment.

Sarah turned to him and looked lovingly into his eyes, gently drawing his chin upward with her soft hands until their eyes met.

"Do I really have to die,

Sarah? Can't you make me well? I feel better now that you are here. Can't I feel this way all of the time?" Timmy was choking back the tears as he asked, the old fears suddenly gripping his mind once again.

"No, Timmy. Before you came to Earth, you chose to live only nine years in this lifetime."

"You came to teach your parents to accept death as a natural process, that death is nothing to fear. You are a brave little boy."

"Your parents have always feared death in other lifetimes. Now it is time for

them to understand, and they in turn will help other parents understand about death — other parents whose children are dying as you are."

Sarah's words were like a light bulb flashing on in Timmy's head.

"Oh, I see," said Tim. "I am kind of a teacher! Wow!"

"Yes," replied Sarah lovingly, "and a great teacher you are indeed! I couldn't do a better job myself."

"Sarah, there is only one thing that makes me sad now," said Timmy, his face beginning to droop again.

"What is that, Timmy?" asked Sarah, hiding the fact

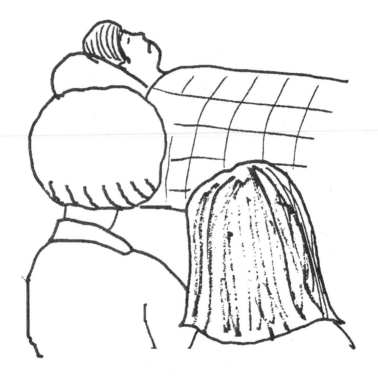

she already knew what he was going to ask.

"How am I going to help my parents understand? How am I going to make them understand what death is all about? Can you help me?" begged Timmy, his voice now beginning to quiver with pain.

"I will help, Timmy. I will help them understand," Sarah assured him.

Tim felt relieved. He laid his head back on the pillow, and as Sarah gently drew the soft comforter up around his chin, Tim quickly fell into a deep sleep, a peaceful glow about his face.

The next day Tim was

feeling much worse. His worried parents sent for the doctor and waited at Tim's bedside for the doctor to arrive.

They were very apprehensive about Tim's condition, knowing in some way that he was about to leave them. Tim's mother was clinging tightly to his frail arm, not willing to let go for fear she would never see her little boy again.

For a few moments, Timmy opened his eyes and spoke in a very faint voice. "Mom, Dad, please don't cry. Don't feel bad about me leaving.

"I am going to a beautiful

place. My guardian angel came last night; her name is Sarah.

"Sarah showed me where I will go after I die, and she promised to help you both understand, too. The angel told me to tell you good-bye.

"I have to go now, so other people can learn not to be afraid to die. You can help them understand because you will understand when Sarah shows you what she showed me. You will understand when you go to the bridge in the garden."

"Grandma is there," Timmy continued, "and Aunt Fay . . . Uncle Jack, too. And

best of all, Jesus is there."

"Jesus said He would be waiting for me, He would stay at the bridge and wait for me to come. He said I would not be alone, and that I would never again be sick and in pain."

"Please be happy, for me!"

Tim's parents looked at each other in a puzzled glance, tears streaming down their cheeks at the thought of their child's death, his leaving them.

Then a beautiful golden white light slowly filled the entire room. A warm, loving glow filled their hearts.

"Sarah, you came back,"

whispered Timmy in a very weak voice.

"Yes, Timmy. I am back to help you and your parents as I promised. And I brought along someone very special to help, too."

Tim's parents could not move for a moment in their surprise. Sarah had asked Jesus to accompany her on this journey, and here He was.

Sarah and Jesus helped Timmy's parents see the same pictures Timmy had seen the night before. They saw and talked to Grandma, Uncle Jack and Aunt Fay. And soon, they understood.

Soon they accepted death

as a perfectly natural part of life. They even understood what they were shown about the lifetimes they had shared with Timmy before.

Yes, Jesus and an angel were right here in this very room. They acknowledged among themselves that this was no dream. This was very real. Soon Timmy's parents felt at peace with what was about to take place for their only child.

At the moment his parents accepted his death, at the moment love and peace filled their hearts, Timmy closed his eyes. He knew his parents would pass on the information

from this beautiful experience
to other parents who were
about to experience the death
of their child. He knew his
parents' story would help
others a great deal.

With that thought, Timmy
smiled.

With a beautiful smile on
his face and a golden glow
about his entire body, Timmy
slowly left his physical body.

He began to float, as he
had done before. Only this
time, as he began to float
higher and higher and up and
out of the room, Jesus and
Sarah were there, each taking
one of Timmy's hands.

In what seemed but a

moment, they stood at the end of the crystal bridge in the garden. The garden was alive with colors, as if to celebrate Timmy's arrival.

"You may cross the bridge now, Timmy," said Jesus with a beautiful smile.

"Yes," said Sarah. "It is time for you to cross the bridge, Timmy. We will go with you now to the other side."

Timmy stopped for a moment to look at his brand new body. Yep! A brand new body. No pain. No sickness. No scar on his knee from the bike accident. Just a beautiful new body.

He could feel love all around him — a beautiful, joyful, accepting love. No matter who he was — how small, how insignificant, he was just as loved and accepted as all the others in this wonderful place. He was home!

Timmy almost ran across the bridge to where he was greeted by his grandmother and relatives who had passed on before him.

"Yes, this is truly a beautiful and loving place. I am home, but I wonder, who I will be when I decide to come back to Earth?"

About the Author

The '80s were a decade of self-discovery for Leia Stinnett after she began researching many different avenues of spirituality. In her profession as a graphic designer she had become restless, knowing there was something important she had to do outside the materiality of corporate America.

In August 1986 Leia had her first contact with Archangel Michael when he appeared in a physical form of glowing blue light. A voice said, "I am Michael. Together we will save the children."

In 1988 she was inspired by Michael to teach spiritual classes in Sacramento, California, the Circle of Angels. Through these classes she had the opportunity to work with learning-disabled children, children of abuse and those from dysfunctional homes.

Later Michael told her, "Together we are going to write the Little Angel Books." To date Leia and Michael have created thirteen Little Angel Books that present various topics of spiritual truths and principles. The books proved popular among adults as well as children.

The Circle of Angels classes have been introduced to several countries around the world and across the U.S., and Leia and her husband Douglas now have a teacher's manual and training program for people who wish to offer spiritual classes to children. Leia and Michael have been interviewed on Canadian Satellite TV and have appeared on NBC-TV's *Angels II – Beyond the Light,* which featured their Circle of Angels class and discussed their books and Michael's visit.

The angels have given Leia and Douglas a vision of a new educational system without competition or grades — one that supports love and positive self-esteem, honoring all children as the independent lights they are. Thus they are now writing a curriculum for the new "schools of light" and developing additional books and programs for children.